LETTERS
TO A YOUNG BROWN GIRL

Letters to a Young Brown Girl

POEMS BY
Barbara Jane Reyes

A Blessing the Boats Selection

American Poets Continuum Series, No. 182

BOA Editions, Ltd. ☉ Rochester, NY ☽ 2020

First Edition
20 21 22 23 7 6 5 4 3 2

For information about permission to reuse any material from this book, please contact The Permissions Company at www.permissionscompany.com or e-mail permdude@gmail.com.

Publications by BOA Editions, Ltd.—a not-for-profit corporation under section 501 (c) (3) of the United States Internal Revenue Code—are made possible with funds from a variety of sources, including public funds from the Literature Program of the National Endowment for the Arts; the New York State Council on the Arts, a state agency; and the County of Monroe, NY. Private funding sources include the Max and Marian Farash Charitable Foundation; the Mary S. Mulligan Charitable Trust; the Rochester Area Community Foundation; the Ames-Amzalak Memorial Trust in memory of Henry Ames, Semon Amzalak, and Dan Amzalak; the LGBT Fund of Greater Rochester; and contributions from many individuals nationwide. See Colophon on page 72 for special individual acknowledgments.

Cover Design: Sandy Knight
Cover Art: "An Ally, Isang Alay, at Manananggal (RG)" by Maria Dumlao
Interior Design and Composition: Richard Foerster
BOA Logo: Mirko

BOA Editions books are available electronically through BookShare, an online distributor offering Large-Print, Braille, Multimedia Audio Book, and Dyslexic formats, as well as through e-readers that feature text to speech capabilities.

Library of Congress Cataloging-in-Publication Data

Names: Reyes, Barbara Jane, author.
Title: Letters to a young brown girl : poems / by Barbara Jane Reyes.
Description: First edition. | Rochester, NY : BOA Editions, LTD., 2020. |
  Series: American poets continuum series ; no. 182 | "A Blessing the Boats Selection." | Summary: "Reyes's unapologetic intersectionally feminist "tough love" poems show young women of color, especially Filipinas, how to survive oppression with fearlessness" — Provided by publisher.
Identifiers: LCCN 2020003198 (print) | LCCN 2020003199 (ebook) | ISBN
  9781950774173 (paperback) | ISBN 9781950774180 (ebook)
Subjects: LCGFT: Poetry.
Classification: LCC PS3618.E938 L48 2020 (print) | LCC PS3618.E938
  (ebook) | DDC 811/.6—dc23
LC record available at https://lccn.loc.gov/2020003198
LC ebook record available at https://lccn.loc.gov/2020003199

BOA Editions, Ltd.
250 North Goodman Street, Suite 306
Rochester, NY 14607
www.boaeditions.org
A. Poulin, Jr., Founder (1938–1996)

CONTENTS

BROWN GIRL DESIGNATION

BROWN GIRL MIXTAPE

LETTERS TO A YOUNG BROWN GIRL

☙❧

BROWN GIRL DESIGNATION

. . . bear scant witness to the women who struggled to be heard by their people . . .
—Marjorie Evasco, "A Dream of the Pintadas"

BROWN GIRL FIELDS MANY QUESTIONS

If you want to know what we are whose body parts are scattered to the winds, dispersed as heirloom seeds into the beaks, stomachs, and droppings of migratory birds, broken through our clear film of rage to leaf and fruit, no matter what the territory or terrain,

> *i. In which "you," may indicate a "hearer of unspecified identity," a second person narrator such that the "you," is really meant to be an "I," a "we," regardless of whether the hearer, onlooker, or reader wishes to be included or addressed,*

> *ii. In which "know," may indicate "awareness through observation or inquiry," "having information concerning," "having a personal experience of,"*

> *iii. In which the English "we," is crude, lacking in the specific exclusive and inclusive distinctions of the Tagalog "tayo," and "kami,"*

> *iv. In which "what," is a pronoun choice you might find curious; not "who," which indicates personhood or personified thing, but "what," as in concept, as in phenomenon, as in the object you already believe the "we" is,*

> *v. In which "if," is the operative word, the contingent term, "in case that," "on the condition that," "despite the possibility that," "even though,"*

Here are some questions you may try to consider:

what's it like to be collected and shelved by people who say they dig your (island) (oriental) (tropical) look, your dark lidless eyes, your endless straight black hair,

what's it like for them to tell you with their wide round eyes, how lovely your accent is (they can't identify where it's from though) and yet you still speak such good English (how is that possible),

what's it like to have white people coming up so close, gawking and poking at your flat little nose, your little body, touching your silky hair,

what's it like to hear them tell you 24/7 that they wish they could bottle your skin like a liquid boutique bronzer for that tawny warm glow, all that gold,

what's it like to be this sun-kissed, plump-lipped, almond-eyed, fine-boned tiny thing, to be so precious and treasured and sublime,

what's it like to be so treasured to be trafficked,

what's it like to be locked in for your own good so no one will get their oily fingerprints
    on you, so that no one can hear your soft, soft asking voice,

what's it like when they mispronounce your alien name and shrug, when they tell you
    your ass should be deported,

what's it like when they push you off the sidewalks and into the gutters,

what's it like when they ask if you were bought from a catalog,

what's it like when they mistake you for the help, the nanny, the maid, the janitor, the
    dishwasher, when they say you speak such good English, how is that even possible,

what's it like when they ask whether your mother was a green card hunting whore, a nudie
    dancer near the military base, a drug addict, a welfare cheat,

what's it like when they say you are an illegal, when they say fucking monkey, when they
    ask why you eat dog, when they call you a dirty Filipino,

what's it like when they tell you you should be grateful,

what's it like when white kids in a prom limo yell fucking jap go back to China,

what's it like when big white dudes get in your face shouting anything not white's not right,

who will remind you of Bulosan's songs of love (this meant something to you, once)

who will remind you where the heart is (there, between your third and fourth rib)

who will blame you for effacing your face, for peeling your skin from your body

what's it like when white people yell at you that you ruined the neighborhood because
    you people kept landing at SFO and goddamn Mineta is named after you people
    now, you took over our church, you took over our market, you took over our donut
    shop, you took over our liquor store, you took over our beauty salon with your chatter
    and your babies,

what's it like when they yell at you that you have so many damn babies, now you are
    taking over Silicon Valley and all the schools, and now everything smells like fried
    fish and feet, all the weird shit you people eat, this place was quiet but now your
    gramma's yelling who knows what to your uncles and your cousins, why can't she
    just speak English, fix your busted cars in the driveway parked on the weeds in your
    junk front yard, they're spilling into our street you're parked in front of my home,
    move your damn car, stay away from my daughters, stay away from my dog, fix your
    lawn, this is not the ghetto where you belong,

what's it like when they yell how many goddamn illegals can you pack into that little
    house (fix your paint job; this is not the ghetto), there are so many of you, you've

snatched up all the houses you built over the old orchards you picked the apricots gladiolas and almonds, we remember the mustard flowers and the dragonflies, our children rode their ribboned bicycles, but now your boys racing rice rockets break the quiet into pieces, you killed our peace, you stupid Filipinos can't even drive, what's it like when they say your boys are hoodlums and your sisters are indecent, all your girls are whores, just go back to where you came from, go back to where you came from, go back because you don't belong here, because we never wanted you in our neighborhood

how are you still here, breathing, working, hustling like a motherfucker
how haven't you given up, when everybody tells you not to speak, how are you speaking
how haven't you disappeared into your sheets, into the dark, with the windows shut and the front door bolted
how do you step outside your front door every day, how do you stand and walk that walk
how aren't you afraid, sister, were your parents afraid, how did they teach you to be so steel, please teach me how to be steel like you

BROWN GIRL GHOST

> *. . . María Clara, who was weeping beside an image of the Virgin . . .*
> —José Rizal, *Noli Me Tángere*

A ghost is a dissolving self posting her millionth bathroom mirror selfie so that she will not dissolve. She is soft-focused, she is airbrushed, she is mood-lit. She is over-exposed and whitened. Her eyelashes extend beyond reason. Her hair is tousled, her pupils dilated for you. She lingers, hoping you will see her. She is all angles, ribcage, wide eyes, duck pout. She sucks in her cheekbones. She holds her breath. She pushes out her chest. Because she is thirsty. Because everyone is her daddy. You don't want to blame her. You blame her. You feel sorry for her. You want to punish her for teasing. You want to exorcise her. You want your saliva on her. You want her on your tongue. You click "like," and "share."

❖

A ghost is a dissolving self who is dissolving because she has little else to do but dissolve. She lingers, as no one has given her permission to leave the room. She waits for them to summon her, to refill their rice, to make their coffee, to bring more beer from the ice box. The game's on, and there are guests. Surely, they will call. She will stand in her corner and fold her hands until they call. She will wait.

❖

A ghost is a dissolving self sequestered in the shadows of others. Here, her silence is given. If she sings, if she sobs, visitors will wonder whether they heard a sound. Others will say it is the wind. They will say no soul is here. She may tip over vases, rattle the window panes, but they will say mice. They will say a speeding truck has shifted the foundation. She is a tiny night tremor, and they are soon lulled back into the amnesia of who cooked their supper, who washed their dishes. That they punished her as she would not shush.

❖

A ghost is a dissolved self stressing about dark circles and eyebags, lingering in places when they didn't know you were really there. They never knew whether you had your own tongue. They never knew whether you ate, had a warm bed, a lock on your door. Did you have a door. Whether you could sleep. They wanted your nightmares. They wanted you to wear trauma on your face, with cosmetic correction, photo-finish perfection.

You brushed your chiseled cheekbones with natural pearl powder. In a halter top, the angles of your shoulder blades had runway strut chic. You did this because you thought it made them see you.

❖

A ghost is a dissolving self whose body is sucked of all essence and fight. Wisps where luscious tresses once buoyed by air. Open sores where follicles and bits of flesh have been pulled and pulled again. Eye sockets gaping, irises scratched and dulled. So much hanging skin. Varicose veins, fat spiders overrun the calves. Shells of dead beetles where once cashmere cooed and purred. Chalk and mothballs where dormant orchids once bloomed from all cavities. It is icy wherever she is. Her lipstick has feathered. Mascara and salt in clumps. All sags and wilts. Why is she still here. Why hasn't she disappeared.

❖

A ghost is a dissolved self stressing about what to wear to her own dissolution. In a backless evening dress, every segment of your spine shows. If they see your scars, they will want you to present every terrible detail. Serve these to them with the banquet you have prepared. Let them savor the fragrant steam of you, jasmine tea, coriander, bamboo. Your bones have been simmering so long, your meat just melts away. You render your fat with love, and ladle yourself into their open mouths.

(The elders are polishing pebble and pearl amulets for you.) (The elders want to know when will you start singing lovesongs again.) (The elders are praying the rosary for you.) (The elders want to know when they may lead you back to water.)

Brown Girl Looks in the Mirror

Whereas these apothecaries carry chemical white, poison white, aisles and aisles of jars and mercury vials, bars of papaya soaps stacked up, up high to the light of heaven,

Whereas the butt can be lifted, the breasts implanted, the body liposuctioned and sculpted, the tummy tucked, the nose arched and pointed, the eyes hazel-lensed, lidded, and rounded,

Whereas one may stop eating, and one may airbrush the eyebags, the soft belly, the saddle bags, the cellulite thighs,

Whereas every Daly City tita, every hustling housewife you think to be squirreling away dollars, departing SFO on holiday, returning weeks later as if shellacked, as if sandpapered, as if soaked in chemical baths that dissolve the aged body to its freshest pink,

Whereas every gleaming, newly sharpened nose, every new eyelid blinking, every dermabrasion, every skin so newborn, could instantly blister upon leaving five-star cocoons, into the noxious diesel air of the third world, could bruise blue upon lightest impact, the bustle of departing bodies in international terminals, could desiccate with prolonged exposure to aircraft cabin air,

Here, let it be known that I've arrived at SFO, dark-eyed and flabby, lips peeling, I'm wheeling seventy pounds of pasalubong into the un-glamour of graveyard shifts, where I catwalk in work clogs, my cracked hands princess waving under fluorescent flickers,

Here, see my skin still reptile, and here, see my roots are white.

BROWN GIRL CONSUMED

Dear Brown Girl,

This is just to say, motherfuckers love your food!

Bon Appetit says the latest craze is popcorn and Gummi Bears in your halo-halo, and you're
    looking at this sideways as others nod in gratitude,

Andrew Zimmern also swears by sisig, you're the latest craze, you're an episode of *Bizarre*
    Foods,

He says Americans can't get right with creamy pig brains, so he alters your recipe to make
    it acceptable,

He exits the metropolis in search of the authentic, he slurps worms dipped in vinegar, pulled
    straight from a fucking tree, and then he pales at your "dirty" ice cream. What a dick.

You are *Parts Unknown*, and so Anthony Bourdain also comes to bat for your balut. He throws
    back his head and swallows Emily Dickinson's beaked and feathered hope,

Next time, he'll sip this strange little salty bird, he'll crunch this little baby's bones, wipe
    his mouth, and the world will learn Filipinos are so poor they'll eat anything, a people
    with so much resilience—

Your archipelago is a culinary adventure! You should be so grateful! You are on our map!

Remember when your classmates teased your stinky lunch, your marrow bones, soup, patis,
    and rice, your spoon and fork,
Remember when they told you that you eat dog food, and you didn't know how to go home
    and cry to your mom because she was just too busy working—

Well, fuck all that, because now you're cool,
you're pork bellies sizzling in cast iron cool, you're organic free trade leche de coco
    simmering cool,
you're edgy piquants and aromatics, you're umami, you're pricey specialty grocery items,
    spilling out of the suburban supermarket's ethnic aisle,

you're urban food trucks at an art show cool, you're vegan man bun hipster cool, you're
  deconstructed lumpia cool,
you're wine pairings light-years from the go-to passé Rieslings (yawn),
you're cooler than California rolls, than chop suey, and people freaking the fuck out over
  kung pao chicken at Panda Express don't know how cool you are (they're gag reflexing
  at the innards we third worldlings eat)—

They'll never know the 12-hour workshifts of TNTs sweating into high-end catered
  meals for lesser than minimum wage, under the table, nevermind subsistence,
they'll never know about street kids scrounging for pagpag,
they'll never know the recipes of our cataracted grammas who stayed home and never
  learned to read, or the ones who can still recite José Rizal's "Mi Último Adiós," from
  the heart as the nilaga stews,

Dios mío! The tsismis around tables of itchy gabi leaves and roots and malunggay fronds,
  elders' manicured hands like luya (sige na, anak, they say, clean these tables and we'll
  play mah-jong later),
Dios mío, talaga! Our spinster titas, who singlehandedly took the sharpest machetes to the
  pigs' (and to some men's) throats, bled those tasty motherfuckers, flipped handrolled
  tobacco with their tongues, with their chorus of boning knives, these works of art
  no metropolitan museum would ever show,
Dios mío! All the breaking necks and bleeding, all the flaying and the cutting, in pambahay,
  tsinelas, gold rings, anting-anting. All this after morning mass, all this before noon.
  This is where you told them about your broken heart, this is where they said, ay
  babae, he was never good enough for you. This is where they wiped away your tears,
  and said, anak, you are a good girl,

Fuck these first world gourmands swearing Filipino cuisine is the next big bandwagon to
  ride to the bank, fuck their rebranding for bourgeois Western palates,

Fuck all that, girl, go on get down with your kamayan and your banana leaves, your slurping
  fish heads, your extra rice to soak up the crab butter, your chicharon and San Miguel
  with your crooning titos, your dad's canned Ligo sardines, salted eggs and tuyo cooked
  on the backyard grill, your green mangoes with ginisang bagoong, dear deep red, so
  sweet, so cool.

BROWN GIRL BEGINNING

Dalaga

The breaking begins before you have words for it. Before skinning your knees on sidewalks riding two-wheelers, before coloring books and peachy flesh Crayolas, before Hello Kitty and Disney princesses, before applying your mom's Avon lipstick behind the locked bathroom door, before unearthing your dad's *Playboy* magazines at the back of his closet, before your Barbie dolls' first girl on girl action. They are already breaking you. When your "uncles" kiss you too close to your lips, and inhale you. It doesn't matter how boozy and pomaded, how tobacco-stained or how much gold they're flashing, how much unbuttoned chest hair, aftershave, and body funk. You must allow them to handle you fast at the waist, be a big girl squirming on their laps and bulging crotches. You are to sit still, and smile. When they marvel at how you have grown, *dalaga na*, you learn you are to say, *salamat po.*

Bleed

This is how it began: When I was seven, I never knew that ladies' hands could hold hammers and hurt. When I was eight, they told me to stay in the shade. They told me no man would ever want a dark Igorot girl, so dirty. When I was nine, I learned I should smile at all the men who told me I was pretty. When I was ten, I learned to flip my hair, to roll up my skirt at the waist. When I was eleven, they told me my legs were fat, my knees so black. When I was twelve, they said (in front of company), hija, you should be bleeding na.

Tomboy

When I was twelve, I wanted sharp pressed suits —David Bowie, "Modern Love." I wanted those cheekbones. I wanted to play electric guitar, slung low between my legs, pointing to heaven and wailing. I wanted a motorcycle jacket, and rockabilly hair. I wanted dragon ink to ribbon my arms—Japanese, whiskered, breathing fire. I wanted cowboy boots and a big-ass black Stetson. On Saturday mornings, my dad would call from under his Mustang, '64-½, with Alabama plates. I'd wear his old shirts. I'd hand him each greasy tool, one by one. He'd nod, "that's my boy."

Becoming

When I was thirteen, they let me dance with boys, five, six years older than me. When I was fourteen, they told me I gained weight. They told me my hips were wide. When I was fifteen, they told me I should be a wife by the time I turn twenty-one. When I was sixteen, they told me to study hard and go to college. They told me to stay away from boys. They told me to let the men drive. They told me to wait. When I was seventeen, they told me I must give my parents grandkids. When I raised my eyebrows at them, they told me to do as they say. They told me a lady does not talk back. They told me a lady always obeys.

Cut

After I stopped wearing skin-tight, backless, Lycra minidresses and black cherry lipstick to class. After rolling my eyes and crying a lot, I learned to say fuck you. I set my ex-boyfriend's stuff on fire. I scared the hell out of my roommate, who'd been playing house with some ugly white boy. He drove a shiny car. He bought her shiny things. They convinced me to douse the flames, just ditch my ex's stuff in a public locker downtown. When I cut off all my hair, with blunt scissors in our gray basement apartment bathroom. Swilling Absolut, blasting The Cure's *Disintegration* on my boombox. No, I never cut myself. Yes, I dropped out of college. No, I did not eat. When I wore nothing but the torn-up black 501s that lived on my bedroom floor, ten-eye, second-hand Dr. Martens, some old black T-shirt. When I learned to chain-smoke. When the black circles appeared under my eyes. When I became too old to run away, I just stopped calling home.

Run

One day, a group of boys said they'd rape you. Just drag you behind the bushes, and rape you. Just like that. Because you did not smile at them. Because you did not say thank you. The threat was so artless, and this is when you knew it was idle, dumb boys puffing out their chests because there was nothing else to do that day. Who knows what they were waiting for you to do. When you told them that they could go fuck their mothers (among other things), you could see the fraying, those thinning tethers to manhood, that thing that tells a young man to weep is weakness. Some tears fell. They weren't yours. Nobody touched you that day, not a hand on your motorcycle leather, your fishnet thighs, your shaved skull. Your eyeliner never smeared or ran. You never ran. And even today, you tell this story, only in second person.

Brown Girl Breaking

Tradition

Remember when they said, until a boy is born to a couple, they must not stop bearing children. It is tradition. They meant you were surplus. Remember when they said to your face, no brothers, such a shame. It's too bad you weren't born a boy. You must then know useful things. Clear the table. Do the dishes. Sweep the floors. Babysit. Cook the rice (measure the water up to the first knuckle; don't you know that already). It's too bad you are not pretty; you will never marry a doctor, they said. You will never have mestizo children, they said. Ay, babae, they said. Ay, sayang, they said.

María Clara

Remember when they said, why can't you be more María Clara, more true, Filipina. More model of modesty, more model of grace, they said. A fresh rose, opening. A dewdropped angel. More child. More los ojos sonríense. More chrysalis. More waiting for permission, they said. Why can't you be more blushing, more tremulous. Más tierno el amor. Why can't you be more weepy, faint, contoured, dimpled. More soft spun silk. Why can't you be more gazing, solitary, deferent, they said. More brokenhearted. More dulce es la muerte. Motherless, warded, shredded, and wet. 'Susmarya, they said. Why can't you be more like that, they said.

Sampaguita

Remember when they said, hija, why can't you be more sampaguita, model of fidelity, model of devotion. More white, more aromatic. More starry-eyed. More versatile. Opened at dusk. May you be farmed, collected, propagated by gentle cutting. May you be susceptible to attack. May dirty hands string you together. May coins exchange hands in the speeding streets for you. Why can't you be more self-sacrificing. More promise making, sumpa kita. You may be small. You may not be showy. If we may use you in all the ways we wish, then you will be more lovely to us.

White

Ay, Dios mío, your nose is so flat, your little chinky eyes, your hair like a bruja. Others would bleach and operate to get rid of what you got. Others would die. You're so awkward and bony. Your children will look like little monkeys. You're so dark, you look dirty. Just being dark, no one will want you. You're so ugly. Ay, salamat sa Dios, prize the God-given sharpened nose, the wonder-filled luminous eyes, the soft, baby-brown hair. Others would bleach and operate to get what you got. Others would die. You're so tall and slender. You will have such angelic children. Eternally white, you are confident. Just being white, you win. You're so delicious.

Sour

Remember when they said, you need a man to complete you, to fill you, yes, to fill you till you can no longer be filled. To give you sons. To give you worth. To make you cry. To trophy you. To show you what's good. If you are alone, people will suspect. They will ask each other why you have been overlooked, sour milk left on the shelf to spoil. They will voice their own theories, why no man wants you. Try not to be so difficult. You need a man to make decisions for you—what to eat, how much. What you must and must not wear (in what size, siyempre). When you may speak, what you may say. Whom you must forgive. For whom you must bend. When you must absorb all the blows. When you must absorb all the blame.

Lady

A lady does not open her own doors. A lady does not leave the home without first asking permission. She does not voice her opinions or contradict. She does not frown, smirk, or slouch. A lady does not quarrel in public, place her needs before others, or perspire. She does not monopolize the conversation. She does not invite, initiate, or compete. A lady does not remove her shoes in public. She does not use her hands. She does not laugh, shout, or scratch. She does not swear or smoke. She does not belch, fart, piss, or shit. She does not coordinate her own movement. A lady does not mind. A lady does not eat. A lady does not matter.

Bend

Remember when they said, you must never slouch, ladies. You must always bend. When a bamboo reaches its highest peak, it bends back down to the soil. Elegant, effortless. Bend. Slender, there, at the waist, cambré. To bend is an art. Allongé, let wind, let waves pass through the vertebrae, and sway. Bend at the nape with grace. No matter the strain or weight, accept that you must allay. And the body will be a haven they claim. The bamboo bends. It does not break. To break is common. A lady is not common. You must always save face. You must not let them see you break.

Break
When they tell you, you belong by his side. You are his lady. What will happen when you ask for space. What will happen when you try to leave. He will come after you. Yes, he will come. You will be returned to him. You will always be returned to him. Or you will burn. You will always be his lady. You belong to him, belonging. Please do not argue, please do not overreact. There is nothing you can say. You will be OK, if you keep your head down. If you do not ask. If you do not speak. You must stay. You must. Smile. You must smile that lovely, lipsticked smile.

Remember to arm yourself. Remember to make a break.
And by any means necessary, remember to not look back.

BROWN GIRL HUSTLE

Grind

I see you, running from job to job, hustling up shit-stained escalators. Your discount store black patent comfort shoes are killing your feet. You're boarding the train invaded by white manspreading assholes. You're elbowing your way through turnstiles and messenger-bagged tech bros, you're sardining into piss-rank buses. This is where you're eating your lunch. You'll forget to reapply your lipstick. Your eyebrow wax is two weeks overdue; what a mess your face is. You're graying. You don't have time for color correction. I see you fingering your hemline. You're thinking your skirt's a tad too short. Your control top pantyhose is starting to run. Your hair bun's coming undone. I need to tell you I see you. You're never not running. You're never not working. They act as if you are not even here. They erase you. But I see you. Yes, I see you. I know it'll be dark when you sit, just for a minute in the kitchen, when you take a deep breath, when you begin again.

Playaz

See us? We are the last Pinays standing, in this smoke-stained place, the bourbon no better than high lead level tap water. If there are still jukeboxes filled with scratched 45s, they belong right here. We're young but not too young, we're out past curfew. Your eyes see little brown ball-bangers in this valley of tables. You peek down our blouses, you press up as we bend. We know we got you beat, man. Our shots are clean, we kiss only when we mean. Go ahead, break. Your body english tells us we'll be sinking gold. Halika, see what we can do with this stick.

Ana (Swing)

See how we do not tap out. We slide our way out of your hold. We spring back up when you sucker punch. We bite down so hard, our mouths break tin and tart inside. When we get back up, you mispronounce our names. Still. We'll correct you, sometimes. We all pick our battles. When we speak up, you step back, big stance. We bend our knees, we open our hips. Pivot, and there's our left jab in your jaw. We bob and weave, we block and swing. Right cross, left hook. We are not too dainty for this grappling and grounding. We don't care if you don't like what we're wearing. We'll take you down, we'll choke you out. And then we'll walk.

Pia (Queen)

Brother, see how I roll lumpias wearing this tiara, this much mascara, and my fave black super skinny jeans. I shoot selfies with millionaire ballers. They are starstruck in my sequined glow. My eyebrows are so sharp, they slice you so clean, you don't have time to remember to bleed. I sprint up your mountains in my five-inch pumps. I trained myself in seven. I leave you in the dust.

I step into the room; elders' looms get clacking. Clopping cobblestone. Swishing silk. And how my genteel countrymen swoon. My jusi couture, my capiz shell terno, my siete cuchillos, if only María Clara could have cut with these. My evening gown's a river plunging, you cannot fathom its depth. Gemstones shined by typhoon, by rush, by the rawest force of will.

You cannot airbrush me. There is no need. You cannot translate me. I command your tongue. I thwack your knuckles with my curling iron, when you do not step back. I sing karaoke, loud, and off key. No, you really cannot quiet me.

Brown Girl Glossary of Terms

Internal Colonialism

In the story, children who bite their tongues eat a porridge of falsehood 'til they are fattened little piggies. In the story, ladies who say yes are locked in wrought, jeweled cages. They sway to the tune of Taylor Swift covering Earth, Wind & Fire, and they say, this is fine.

Decolonization

They want to take this word away from you. They want you to explain why you look Asian, when your name is clearly Spanish. They want to bring you Jesus, even though they see your people nailing themselves to crosses on Good Friday. Moreover, they think they brought you light bulbs, feminine hygiene products, and feminism. They love your fine white sand beaches. They think your whole nation is military bases and air-conditioned shopping malls, and fine white sand beaches made for them. They need you to clean their houses and raise their babies. They don't even pay you minimum wage to change their elders' adult diapers. They don't accept that you are from Oakland. They don't accept that you have a nation they did not name.

White Privilege

In the story, the hero is always light-eyed and fair-haired. The distressed damsel is as well. Of course, he is meant to claim her. Of course, they are meant to have the brightest babies. See them banish all dark from their domain. See them build their castles of light where our dark children play. Our dark bodies and tongues will be outlawed. Our dark gods as well. See the hero thrust himself upon his dark maidservants. See those dark maidservants shushed. See how wretched and ratchet, all their dark bastards, ruckus making hoodlums and hooligans. See the hero and the damsel call the cops. Hear the chorus of "not all white people." Hear the chorus of "all lives matter." See the waterfall of white tears.

Pinoy

You know what annoys me? People who won't see the through line from Joe Bataan to Bruno Mars. You ever wonder about the sound of a poet rappin' with ten thousand carabaos in the dark? You ever eat fish and rice with your hands, off Styrofoam plates, in a hole in the wall, south of Market Street? You ever roll down your windows while speeding down Highway 101, to smell the Pajaro River? What if that's the poem, and you missed it, because you were looking for something roseate, effete, something that smells like prestige?

Pinay

Do you know yourself, Pinay? Do you name yourself, Pinay? This name was made here, born here, American as you, your SPAM cans, and your balikbayan boxes. American as the jeepney. American as your father's favorite Applebee's on Farwell in Fremont. Do you cringe when your people don't translate—have you googled "cultural cringe"? I fucking hate that term. Do you know that Prego commercial daughter, pleading, "English please," for her white lover, at a table full of titas and pinsans? That fabled Filipina hospitality, so much giving unto others until you are shoeless, penniless, mute, and hollowed out. Hija, you ain't Jesus, multiplying fishes and loaves.

Pakikipagkapwa-tao

Hella indigenous, which does not mean gone native. Kakayahan umunawa sa damdamin ng iba, for real. You know, like Ruby Ibarra and one hundred Pinays giving you resting bitch face. You know, like those syndicated, full-color photographs, of boys and men in LeBron James and Steph Curry jerseys, thinned flip-flops on their feet, one body together, shouldering a nation. One bamboo hut at a time. One set of lungs breathing. One heart. Isang mahal. Isang bagsak.

Brown Girl Manifesto: #allpinayeverything

Because so much depends upon the suppression of us, the erasure of us, the omission of us; because we are not made to scald, to starve, to stuff in closets; because we have our own lyrics to drop; because we inherit our mothers' immodest tales;

Because our nests and nooks hold buttons, stones and string, pressed flowers, feathers; every rosebud, every bead, every tarnished charm, every scrap of paper nestled between rosaries, safety pins, and scapulars—there are always poems here;

Because so much depends upon the blaming of us, for birthing too many babies, for birthing none at all; because the unruled pages of this body refuse to be marked and ripped in two; because we bind our own perfect spines;

Because of the low hum soothing the lungs, thrum in the throat, buzz in the skull till the head is numb, the body is a chamber of echoing song; scars are stories, healed fractures are as well (this, of course, you've heard before), but not all scars are bodily;

Because we are razor-tongued (this, of course, you've heard before); because we've been told since the beginning of time to hold the tongue lest we lose it; because we still recoil at tendered words; because we remember the water's lullaby;

Because we are a nation of the wretched and the occupied; we reclaim our elders' taken tongues, cut, and burned; because our foremothers were taken, cut, and burned too; and so we offer words, verses to warm, a balm;

Because so much depends upon white nonsense and white fragility, orientalists, white microaggression, white supremacists with their shotguns and tiki torches; because telling us we don't fucking belong is an old and tired story;

Because our being, our breathing, our speaking were never guaranteed; because our father's bones rest in this land and we have grieved; no, I will never leave this place, and no, I will never leave him; because his roots, this land are also mine;

Because so much depends upon vacuous speech, and so sometimes it is best to refrain from all human voice; because when we sit with ourselves, there is just air, just light, and this is how we will learn to listen—

Brown Girl Mixtape

How we sing, even as we are boiled alive.
—Fatima Lim-Wilson

Track: "Gaze," Sweetback, feat. Amel Larrieux (1996).

Squeeze your hand into a fist. Now, loosen, just a bit.
                    They say that is the heart, heat, fiber, sugar. Cut
          around its core, score and invert. Take your teeth
                    to its golden flesh and bite. They say this is the heart
          of a lovely girl. In these stories, there is always a girl,
lovely as that dream just before waking. There is always
                    a girl, whose dainty feet make light where she toe-taps
          the earth, so soft. Elders tell her patience will saint her.
And so she waits. There is always heartbreak, chambers
                    washed in longing, pulsing dark inside the body. She waits.
They say she waited with the waning moon, until the dawn.
                    She waited. Press your index finger and tall finger
                              into the underside of your jawbone, and count.

TRACK: "MY LIFE," MARY. J. BLIGE (1994).

Back in the day, we burned white sage, we filled our small spaces with lavender and sunlight. We were such love thirsty brown girls, aching, unslaked. How do you fill a vessel of want.

Back in the day, always on the edges, looking into others' tidy white lives. When we subsisted on cheap tea and nicotine, when our belongings, mostly poem-filled notebooks, fit neat into milk crates.

Back in the day, we wished to be so beautiful in our darkness. We occupied nowhere, stared into spaces we didn't think we'd belong. We walked if we didn't have bus fare. If you look at our lives back in the day, you will see such sad girls, so much unmet grace.

Track: "Blackwinged Bird," Emm Gryner (2006).

We won't hold our tongues fast.

We won't unforget all we've been made to stuff back into our darkest places and sew shut.

We know the heart heals with time, and that bruises heal too.

We know how to leave a boy who hurts with words or fists.

We know how to ghost a boy who doesn't even deserve our ghost.

We know how to change numbers and locks, that sometimes behind a bolted door, the
    only thing that will keep us company is a good record collection and fire.

We remember not to say sorry.

We know some boys do not deserve a proper good-bye.

Track: "A Girl in Trouble (Is a Temporary Thing)," Romeo Void (1984).

Brown Girl Sings Whalesong
When they say you are as big as a lumpy, blubbery whale,
                    you may go ahead and bellow deep. Creak,
          croon, and trill, moan low. Go ahead, open your mouth so wide, that
                         you can swallow the sea. Know that your blood pulls you through
what your oldest ancestors committed to heart. Remember
            you have touched the ocean floor, and you have made your garden there.
                    Remember, your skin is thick. Remember, no one has tamed you.
                         Yes, you are immense, your lifespan and memory long,
your heart larger than a full-grown man. Your lungs carry air for us all.
            Your ribcage could be a refuge. Your skull is a cavern of deep song.
                         Through murk and poison, you move true with the moon.
Your body lights a million lanterns. Your deep pitched song finds your sisters,
                    your mother. They say the earth's most unruly parts sing like you.

TRACK: "ICE AGE," HOW TO DESTROY ANGELS (2012).

There is always a brown girl who knows exactly how and when to open up the walls and disappear. We know this is easy as breathing on a cool day. We know how to pluck music from the air, and how to pluck away grays. We know how to call for ocean to rise, cold salt and tide, how to bury, and how to build fire. We know we are that ocean. We know how to strip away sound, pulse, and subside. From barely a sigh, we can hold a pure note high. We know that to be a brown girl is to call the ocean is call to the self is to know you have to find a way.

TRACK: "DAHIL SA IYO," PINAY (1998).

Do you know how old you were when you first saw the ocean,
How old you were when the ocean first touched you,
How old you were when you knew you were the ocean.
Do you remember its cradle and nudge, its pull and boom, your skin shocked by your
    own pinpricks and ice, do you remember sinking.
How were you ever so new, swaying into something so immense, so beyond sight.
Do you remember tasting slip, sand, and swell.
How were you ever anything but a siren singing sea in woman skin, gliding in quiet, light
    filtered through bluegreen filtered through plastic and shard.
Do you remember the rocks. How old were you when you returned.

Track: "Orange Moon," Erykah Badu (2000).

We are always the light, fireflies circling 'round the star apple trees.

How good it is to be this sweet, smoldering light.

How good it is, to be this sun setting fire to the bay, gleaming off glass, diamonds before the dusk. Girl, we are gems cut so keen and fine. How we cut.

How we hum honey, open the lungs, the throat, and our song a chorus of praise and day. We glimmer so bright.

How good it is, to be so bright, to pay no mind to those who don't abide, so many who would dull our shine.

Track: "Drop," Hope Sandoval & the Warm Inventions (2001).

What are the things that tear up your language, what are all the things that make you bite your tongue to be bloodless. Drop them all, stone by stone and resound. Tune your vocal chords, slough away the layers of white noise. The sting when exposed anew. Smooth the creases in your voice's scraps and crumpled pages, soothe and strum. Sometimes, when we hear a murmur, a hum, we forget that is us. Sometimes, we get down, and sometimes, the throat is tender as waking for Sunday morning mass.

Track: "You're the One," Fanny (1971).

Hell yeah, let this Brown Girl sing because I know what I know and I know what I need.

I know there's no roadmap, no neat paved ways for someone like me.

I'm going anyway. Watch me go. I'm going to draw my own map. I'm going to lead me to myself.

I see some avenues, then everyone blocks my path, catcalling chickadee, cooing babydoll.
    They call me wild honey flower. They want to touch my hair.

Hell nah! I'm singing, hear me spin and weave lyrics with these woman hands, hangnails and all.

Hell yeah, let this Brown Girl be, ruby rock and roll gypsy in a big man's big dirty world.

I make ovaries of stone. I make the hottest blood. I'm the one. I'm my own thing.

Track: "Blood Moon," Low Leaf (2016).

All I have enters into moonlight, calling to fill you, tangling you earthbound, my many branches transcribing dark rooting of lungs bellowing, limbs combing, psalms humming, earth to limbs to hair to split ear to fingers to listening tree trunks who pull ebony and magic from autumn air, who string psalms into feet and belly and tongue, and you are all I have to enter into moonlight, and you are the trees of my song, of my throat trilling through a body calling me to you, a bird song that hovers then needles through ancient places, a deep blue bellow that is a song returning to the loam.

Track: "Sonrisa," Si*Sé (2001).

Sister, doesn't your face hurt from smiling all the time.
So does mine. When we are supposed to blossom and smile,
let's wail low instead. We'll wail so low, and so long.
Under the breath, so quiet, we'll spell. We are so tiny to their eyes.
Time will move, and time will push us all along,
and they will forget we are there, as speck, as germ, as lurking, as dark.
We are a tinted tongue of tiny heat. If you want to know how to break the big—
sometimes, we are the spore, and sometimes, sister, yes, we are the spark.

TRACK: "FIREWOMAN," BARBIE ALMABIS (2005).

There is more of me to hear than this grooved edge. Hear my voice break.
Even the poem, how it is a hot golden thing peeled from me,
quiet and packed, amber and thick. This cut wax track, this edged light,
this almost whisper, this honeycomb harvest, this sweet hiding in plain sight.
Yes, this is me, cut and wrecked and more. Hear me.
Yes, this is my want, packed edge to edge to edge.
I am the beautiful thing poised timeless in amber, ready to break it open.

TRACK: "DEVOTED," JULIE PLUG (2001).

Watch me as I take a heart, she says. Bare-handed, pull apart the fibers, and make sure to catch the juice. My unwed aunties taught me how to undress a fresh heart. First, peel away the rough husk—this is not work for tender hands. Take care not to touch its itchy sap. The heart is fragrant, and it is durable. You may brine a heart, or you may braise a heart. You will see how a heart softens. You may mince, spice, and serve a well-seasoned heart.

Do not pluck it unripe. Wait until it wants to open.

TRACK: "KADKADDUWA," GRACE NONO (2008).

Brown Girl Has Walked into the Wild, Palms Open
　　　　　See how she lists. The body is bent as light, as wind will it.
And so you must tread light. Mind the rocks underfoot. You must tread slow.
There has been drought; see where water has long ago troughed, has carved her.
　　　　　See how she branches, twisting, her many hands reaching.
Her roots also reach, sweetened from reaching. When fire arrives, she toughens.
She will slough away the thick. She will be slick, and dark beneath the rough.
She will mimic the fire her bones remember. Know her bones glisten.
　　　　　See how she rests. The body will fall, as time wills it.
See how it hollows, how her pieces return to earth.
　　　　　And from her thick trunk, mushrooms cluster—
　　　　　　　　　　Her belly a nest of moss and poison.
When broken open, see what of her mother she has kept,
　　　　　　　　　　what of her father, what of the stars.

TRACK: "LOVE, PEACE AND HARMONY," BOW WOW WOW (1983).

How I wanted Me bad badass and badly,
    Me, drumming bang bang, Me riot woman booming,
      Me not ornament girl Me
        but one hella glittered self who is your You
    and my I,   no caged little thing, but a wild sparkling You,
            a hella starburst wow,
 and how I wanted Me to be hella starburst wow too,
    how I wanted Me to be You, the rushing, chair throwing I,
        a table flipping heart throbbing,
 and how I wanted Me to be the blistered woman ruckus, banging, booming,
    how I am You, crashing fire woman,
         You not sidepiece You,
  but unpolished goddamn seething human to my Me,
       an ever crushing heart that is my You.

TRACK: "A LITTLE BIT OF ECSTASY," JOCELYN ENRIQUEZ (1997).

Every single thing our titas cannot bear to see.

Every single bit of native skin flashing, island warm, hella not Castilian, hella not
Eskinol, every single bit of not Euro nose, and not Anglo eyes.

Every full hip sway, every long braid whipping around, every body piercing gleaming
golden, every lush stroke, every raised eyebrow, every dark full lipsticked, bronzed
as bourbon and beaming, glorious nape and clavicle bared, every bit of high-heeled
wide stance, fists to open hands.

Every single thing our pearl-clutching titas wished us not to be.

Track: "Fall on You," June and Jean Millington (2011).

Mama how you and your blue mountains twang and strum and twang and strum sounds
    like wind sounds like you turned sorrow done roll throats to you anything you rock
    blue hands water silver all slow wet harmonicas how wild how big and

Mama my smoky Mama see Mama sweet Mama sing Mama sing Mama like you know
    night done up like heat like hair nothing like your sound such spit such listen this
    chorus of old train stations this jam session sounds like salvage

Mama sing see your hands see how this is so much go

TRACK: "SOULFUL DRESS," SUGAR PIE DeSANTO (1964).

We'll shake and we shout 'til morning and roar.
No, there's nothing tamed about us, not the hemline,
not the neckline, not this streak of red lipstick,
not these shit kickers. Nothing silent, nothing shy,
nothing here but fly. Nothing asking nothing from you,
'cept, get outta our way, 'cept this is no ask.
Don't tell us to dial it down. Don't tell us to be ladies.
We'll show you our teeth. Don't lecture that we reckless,
just recognize. You step the fuck back son, and you recognize.

Track: "Bad Girls," M.I.A. (2010).

We (dis)(orient)(al) girls, we all side eye, gasoline, and gravel, yeah.
We gold dust coated, we bad mannered bitches,
we brown, and we drive, and we dirty. Yeah,
we drive dirty, and we call your bullshit bullshit when you say smile,
we spit hard fast, when you say sweet, when you say easy,
we say fuck you, we say fuck you and your orient. Yeah,
we nails and teeth, and you don't want to mess with us.
We full of kick and claw, we full of bite. We say eat our dust,
we say eat our tire tracks, and we say girl, hell yeah. We good.

Track: "US," Ruby Ibarra, feat. Rocky Rivera, Klassy, and Faith Santilla (2017).

Sure as islands rise from the floor of our fiery ocean,
as bone shattering heat, as hunger hollering fists
through windows and shards beneath shell toes
ground into sand as summertime pavement steams,
sure as why we drop lyrics in chorus, in curses, in crescendo,
sure as this is all ours, our ruckus that got you wrecked,
yes, this is ours, hear us wordsmiths worlding, hear us woke,
hear how we got not one ounce of asking,
not one smidgen of sorry from this body of bodies,
sure as our elders' tongues sear into and through us—

sabihin mo na, babae, awitin mo, tulain mo,   *tumayo ka na, babae,*
o, sige na nga babae, nakikita kita, kaya mo,   *bahala ka na, babae.*

LETTERS TO A YOUNG BROWN GIRL

. . . nothing to break or barter but my life / my spirit measured out, in bits . . .
—Diane di Prima, "Revolutionary Letter #1"

Dear Brown Girl,

They will say, your language lacks finesse, your words low. They will form air quotes with their white fingers, say something clever about color. They will corral you into their lowness, as you sully their well-lit high poetic annals. With your darkness. They will say all of these things as they are stealing your language away from you. Until you cannot speak on your own behalf. Until you cannot speak at all. They will say you are simple, making inelegant noise. You are lowing. There is no thievery, they will say, the light is dim in here. You must not trust your own eyes, they will say. See how they cow you. See how they see you (when they wish to see you)—some brown cow best left in darkness.

And I will say, I have mastered your language. I speak it better than many of you monolingual assholes making ching chong noises at me. You think you clever. I know your dirty tricks. I'll throw air quotes when you say, "diversity," and "unity," and "inclusive," when you say, "I don't see race." And I will roll my eyes mighty. Trust this. And I will say everything I say in my many tongues, too much for your mouthing empty words, you don't even know what I'm saying. My noise is inelegant, because I'm throwing f-bombs at you, motherfucker. I don't give a shit if you think it's coarse. Yeah, I'm pretty animal, I'm beastly. Are you threatened that this dark monster can holler and drown you out.

DEAR BROWN GIRL,

After all this, you still ask me how it is I arrived at the poem. I want to tell you about my rounded, looping penmanship in berry scented ink. I want to tell you about typing my words on an old typewriter, pushing its carriage return, poems with no correction tape. I want to tell you about drafts upon handwritten drafts, about the smell and feel of so much cream and marbled Florentine paper, about cutting class and taking the afternoon to shop for handcrafted notebooks and writing implements. I want to tell you about my pink inked lowercase i's, dotted with chubby hearts. I held so much unrequited sweetness. I want to say I was waiting, but I don't know what I was waiting for. So much ache. So much breaking. I want to say so much about silencing and time.

DEAR BROWN GIRL,

Remember those diaries we were gifted as young girls, pale pink and floral, embossed with golden curlicues. Remember that tiny golden lock and precious key. Remember wanting to crawl inside and hide there. Remember how not speaking yielded so many secrets. Remember how you'd write and write, like if you didn't write, you would just die. Like if anyone ever read what you wrote, you would just die. They'd say, artista ka talaga, 'susmaryosep, anak. And you'd cry. Of course you'd cry.

Remember when you were nineteen, your poems were so honey coated. Your language was not really your language. It was so sugary, fancy and high. You wrote about things you didn't know how to write about. Nineteen-year-old girl living on Top Ramen and minimum wage, remember how you blew a whole paycheck on a Waterman Laureat mineral blue fountain pen, and tender purple ink, how you transcribed your finished poems into the matching hardbound, violet marbled journal edged with gold leaf. You loved that scratch of gold-plated nib onto paper. You gazed at each glossy page air-drying before you turned the page or closed the book.

Dear Brown Girl, nobody ever read your poems back then. And then again, none of those poems were for them, di ba?

Dear Brown Girl,

What is there to fear in your silence. When you do not speak, do you hear your own footfalls, your breath, your measured gait, can you feel tension and give of earth with every step. Can you feel how terrain changes underfoot. What does this tell you about the sprawl and tangle of roots, about seeds that open only when fire comes. What happens when you pay attention. What happens when you step outside of words. What do you learn about heartbeat. Can you hear the single leaf fall to the soil. And when there is rustle, through limbs, through hollowed trunks, do you know what living thing moves into the underbrush. Can you see its tracks. Can you catch its scent. If you know how to listen, there is an entire language of water and earth, wings and husks and legs, heat and birth. What do you find when you sit with yourself inside your silence.

Dear Brown Girl,

What if nobody cares, except your brown sister fighting for air as she is trampled underfoot, her hair and clothing pulled by those clawing to hold her back. Your brown sister is tending to what's been broken. She might be concussed. Why should she care for you, when you just knocked the wind out of her.

What if nobody cares, but the three other dark folk crouching outside the room, big-eyed, thirsty like you. How are you going to pretend you didn't claw at them, pull their hair, step all over them, and push yourself forward and into the room. How are you going to make them care about you now. You mistook yourself an honored guest. White people keep telling you to refill their glasses, give their guest rooms a quick tidying up, wash their soiled linens. They proposition you and grab your ass. They are impressed you do not protest. They love your nodding and smiling at exactly the right moments. They are impressed by how well you mimic their tongue. It's like a little song.

DEAR BROWN GIRL,

Do you ever get sick of trying to be a miscast space filler in someone else's self-absorbed narrative, that has nothing to do with you. That whether you are in their room or not, it makes no difference to their outcome, though you add color and spice. Do you ever get so fed up, you just want to flip a table, or throw a chair, say this some bullshit, storm out of the room, and slam the door behind you.

A couple of things about that room. They don't want you in it. It's true. But it's also true that it's a pretty whack ass room. Its outdated décor is garish and overstuffed. The air in their room is dense with mold. And it is filled with people who keep running into you because they don't see you there, or want to suit themselves in your skin, then disrobe and stash you when you become inconvenient, such as when more important people enter the room. This room is also filled with brown people who are okay with being flayed and trashed. When they are not pleading with you to just shut your mouth, they are trying to push you out the window. Why do you want so badly to be in this room with them.

When they try to convince you that they are "not racist but," you can tell them to shut their dirty lying mouths. You can tell them where they can refill their own glasses. See their eyes well up, see how small they become. See them now, disrobed, see them whimper and mewl. You can tell them their fragility is coming unhemmed, peeking out from their yellowed drapes. Their fabric must have been cheaply manufactured. Gaze at them for a short while. You don't even have to say anything mean. Say nothing at all. Just gawk, and occasionally, smile. See the sheen on their Vaselined teeth melt away. See the luster of their precious room disappear.

DEAR BROWN GIRL,

What if nobody reads you, but every young, hungry brown girl who crosses your path. Please let them be visible to you. Their eyes are so wide; they have rarely ever seen a woman like you before. They see you speak like you have forgotten the fear, the harm speaking brings brown women like you, daughters of spilling bodies and sutured mouths. They never knew brown women like you were real, speaking head held high, speaking like you know. Because you know, and because you know that you know. They are holding your words so close to their bodies, the way we were all taught to cradle a newborn babe, like they were taught to hold God's words close to their hearts. They are breathing in your pages. They can't bear to remember what it was like before they found you. What if they are the only ones who ever read you. Would that be so bad.

Dear Brown Girl,

What if I told you that you don't have to do as you're told. Yes, you can cut up the script they made you recite by heart with your cut up tongue. Yes, by those people, who wanted you to be their lace trimmed, pink silk ribboned heart shaped box. Yes, they wanted you to let them open you up, they wanted to slit, split open all your little smooth sweet pieces, to mouth you, to melt you. As if you would just let them. Yes, you are allowed to open, twirl your butterfly-bladed words—siete cuchillos, I see you sister, your swift knives concealed under your lace edged, silk ribboned skirt.

Dear Brown Girl,

We know it's not about not speaking English; Francophones speak French, and all is right in the Global North. We are tropical birds puffing our chests, trilling our Spanish surnames; we roll our Rs as if they were gilded baroque ornaments. And with a hard pop of the lips, we say P not F, B not V. Our mother tongues are tough on the mouth, and spewing spittle, vinegar, and bits of ginger, we make kuwento, all of us, all at once. And sometimes it sounds like a lot of neck bones cracking. And from those neck bones, everyone's bellies are filled. Our kin build beautiful, soulful somethings from a whole lot of nothing. Our kin forage, and from what is deemed low, cultivate light.

Dear Brown Girl,

I. You have come to me, to ask how a brown girl writes and lives, lives and writes, when it feels like no one cares; you have come to ask me whether it is true that no one cares about some brown girl.

2. You have come to me, because you need me to see you.

3. Yes, it is true; if our identities are not for sale, then no one cares about some brown girl.

4. I am sorry if what I say here are not the things you want to hear from me.

5. Some say it is bourgeois privilege for the battleground to be the page.

6. I think the page could be one weapon in our armories.

7. "Diversity," "inclusion," and "multicultural" blunt the narrative.

8. "Patriarchy" and "empire" disorient; "status" and "privilege" pervert our aim.

9. Let's put those words back on the shelf, where they belong.

10. I have no identity to sell; what is mine is precious to me, though others would tell me nothing is mine, not the air in my lungs, not the ground beneath my feet.

11. You may unfollow me on social media if you don't like what I'm saying, and this is OK.

12. You ask for kindred words from me, because like you, my ancestors' words are slowly losing their ground.

13. You have come to me fearing kapwa, hoping I could allay this fear.

14. You have come to me seeking kapwa, hoping I could clarify this sight.

15. I learned that kapwa is seeing the self in others; I think of kapwa as a sanctuary of shared selves.

16. Speakers of our elders' words do not (wish to) see themselves in the flushed and stuttering selves we have become.

17. We can't find the correct idioms fast enough; we no longer know the correct accent marks and glottal stops.

18. We came of age here, silent, witnessing kapwa's erosion and erasure.

19. You want me to affirm that the proper response is outrage; you want me to affirm your outrage.

20. Yes, there is outrage, a heat in my blood; it is a silent, slow, and steady burn.

21. But there is so much sadness, being so torn from my elders and kin.

22. But there is so much noise, so much shouting, so much shouting above the shouting.
23. This is where we start shutting other people up, deciding who gets to speak, and what they get to say.
24. This is where we assign a price to "voice," and who must pay in order to speak.
25. This is where we come to buy and sell voice, and then voice is only for those who can afford it.
26. This is where we invent adages about voicelessness.
27. And we continue to shout the things other people are shouting.
28. And we continue to shout, and it becomes easy to ignore all of this shouting.
29. And we continue to shout, and it becomes easy to pretend nobody is shouting.
30. I want to think we all resist becoming the thing we are shouting at, though this may not be true.
31. How may we honor this thing called voice, and how can we honor our kapwa.
32. I fear all this shouting depletes our loób, which is where the wisdom of our elders has rooted.
33. Conquerors documented this wisdom as superstition, godlessness, the lore of lowly women and unenlightened people.
34. You have come to me asking that I serve as beacon, and now I see we had not previously agreed on what needed illumination.
35. We now busy ourselves with curriculum vitae items, noteworthy mentions, hit counters, hyperlinks, and into social media posts, from glass ceilings, the dropping of names onto unswept gumstuck floorboards which barely cover the dirt.
36. I do not know that our elders envisioned this dim administrative morass for us.
37. You must understand, I thought we came here to discuss "liberation," and now I see we had not previously agreed upon defining the term together.
38. One brown girl's liberation is another brown girl's bloated bureaucracy, monuments of micro-aggression, mansplaining, and migraines.
39. One brown girl's "woke," is another brown girl's mess of vacuous memes and info-bytes, as if these things were precious clean water during centuries-long drought.
40. Why must one brown girl's words doom another brown girl to erasure.
41. Why must one brown girl's words be buried for being too much, for being not enough, for being unlike everyone else's.
42. Can we return to that loób, where there is potential for our cells to grow something other people, we ourselves, do not expect.

43. We can worldbuild, unorthodox, fierce from our loób—their unmapped places—using everything we can get our hands on.

44. Remember our elders were experts at third world improvisation, filling our bellies despite famine, salvaging masterworks from basura; we marvel at how low and few the parts are required for making masterpiece.

45. Let there be no romance, no artifice here; our elders' worldbuilding gave us life.

46. I now see my late father's love for swap meets and junkyards through a different lens; he took the broken, the throwaways, last year's off brand items, inkjet printers, scientific calculators, so many lenses and glasses, digital wristwatches, remote control race cars, landline telephones.

47. He dissembled, he tinkered, and reconfigured these into something else.

48. Sometimes you break open the old thing, if only to find that one reusable part.

49. Sometimes he made art, and some won ribbons affixed to their title plates; this was my father's loób.

50. Sometimes he failed, and we were left with jagged mountains of parts in his garage; this was also my father's loób.

51. He was a master of salvage and scavenge, and we were ashamed of his junk.

52. I want to think this was my father's way of telling us he knew the sheen of prestige in this country dulls.

53. I want to think he knew we could never buy prestige in the first place.

54. I never wanted to agree with him; I fought with him until I could no longer deny much evidence was in his favor.

55. I thought all of my classmates lived in accessorized Barbie Dreamhouses.

56. Arranged tidy inside their Barbie Dreamhouses, lemon oil polished dining sets.

57. I thought all of my classmates lived matching Tupperware lives.

58. Arranged tidy inside their Tupperware, PBJs on uncrusted Wonder Bread.

59. They were whole and wholesome, and we were something else.

60. We learned the words for what they thought we were; we took those words into our bodies and their dull blades hollowed us to incompletion.

61. We were told to translate hiya as shame; others translate it as propriety, a dignity that comes from inside (the loób), and this is a lot different from shame.

62. My father's art pieces were sometimes incomplete, and that itself was the narrative.

63. Let there be no shame in being incomplete.

64. My father's art pieces were sometimes imperfect, and that itself was the narrative.

65. Let there be no shame in being imperfect.
66. I am one of my father's incomplete, imperfect pieces.
67. My father's junkyard scavenge is now my unruly poetic statement, my verse monstrosities, my mixed-up diction.
68. I am trying to assign it order, but most times, it will not abide.
69. People say, why aren't you ashamed.
70. People say, why do you broadcast our shame.
71. People say, why don't you just shut up.
72. People say, why are you still here.
73. People say, why haven't you disappeared.
74. Have you ever been made to feel so little.
75. Have you ever made anyone feel so little.
76. If art is a series of fine lenses, then the shame is not hard to see.
77. Beneath these lenses, we are misfitted parts jammed together, fractured at the edges, dirtied from so much mishandling.
78. Beneath these lenses, we are sad little colonies, hoarding second hand items.
79. Beneath these lenses, we are sad little colonies frantic for our grime covered shelters.
80. See how we are not a smiling, suburban, single-family home owning, TV sitcom nuclear body.
81. Inside the body that is our overcrowded house, our fists have made holes in the walls; our hands throw glass, mismatched plates, any object within reach.
82. Inside the body, heat rises, fibers tear and unravel, vessels collapse; the body shuts down.
83. Inside the broken, dirty, dark people that we are, loób has been torn from us; it continues to be torn from us.
84. This is trauma.
85. This trauma is not a little thing that you can brush off your shoulders.
86. This trauma is not a little thing that makes you interesting and diverse.
87. You wanna smack a smug motherfucker for saying that to your face.
88. If your loób is torn from you, this is an act of terror.
89. If your loób is torn from you, this is not done by an invisible hand.
90. If your loób is repackaged, relabeled, and sold back to you at a premium, send it back.
91. This jagged wound, opened, and salted for others to enjoy how we smart.

92.   This is terror.

93.   At some point, we stop asking who is (as)sa(u)lting us, the pleasure they derive tearing us from our loób.

94.   I think we should start asking again; I think we should start asking why.

95.   Inside the body, roots thicken and tangle to repair us; it may not be pretty, but it will hold us together.

96.   I am not sorry if the things I am saying here are not the things you wished to hear.

97.   You may unfriend me on social media; you may block me on social media, and I will be OK with this.

98.   Maybe loób translates as "heart"; I think the heart is only part of that.

99.   I don't think that we should stop making art from our loób.

100.   Do you?

☙❧

Acknowledgments

Thank you to the editors of the following publications, in which some of these poems have appeared, some in earlier versions: *Academy of American Poets' Poem-a-Day, Amber Flora, Apogee Journal, Best American Poetry Blog, Brooklyn Rail, The Brown Orient, GIANTHOLOGY, Hambone, Maganda, Marías at Sampaguitas, New England Review, NO TENDER FENCES: An Anthology of Immigrant & First-Generation American Poetry, Pilgrimage, Rigorous,* and *World Literature Today.*

Thank you, salamat po, Christine Abiba, Jason Bayani, Arlene Biala, Mayo Buenafe-Ze, Rachelle Cruz, Princess Fernandez, Javier O. Huerta, Edwin Lozada, Lisa Suguitan Melnick, Rashaan Alexis Meneses, Veronica Montes, Urayoán Noel, Conrad Panganiban, PJ Gubatina Policarpio, Vicente Rafael, Ire'ne Lara Silva, Melissa Sipin, Leny Mendoza Strobel, Aimee Suzara, Eileen R. Tabios, Lehua Taitano, Angela Narciso Torres, MT Vallarta, Jean Vengua, Benito Vergara, for intertextuality, kuwentuhan, and kapwa. Thank you always, Oscar Bermeo.

About the Author

Barbara Jane Reyes was born in Manila, Philippines, and raised in the San Francisco Bay Area. She is the author of *Gravities of Center*, *Poeta en San Francisco*, *Diwata*, *To Love as Aswang*, *Invocation to Daughters*, and *Letters to a Young Brown Girl*. She teaches in the Yuchengco Philippine Studies Program at University of San Francisco, and lives with her husband, poet and educator Oscar Bermeo, in Oakland.

BOA EDITIONS, LTD.
AMERICAN POETS CONTINUUM SERIES

Colophon

Blessing the Boats Selection titles spotlight poetry collections by women of color. The series is named in honor of Lucille Clifton (1936–2010) whose poetry collection *Blessing the Boats: New and Selected Poems 1988–2000* (BOA Editions), received the National Book Award. In 1988, Lucille Clifton became the first author to have two collections selected in the same year as finalists for the Pulitzer Prize: *Good Woman: Poems and a Memoir 1969–1980* (BOA), and *Next: New Poems* (BOA). Among her many other awards and accolades are the Ruth Lilly Poetry Prize, the Frost Medal, and an Emmy Award. In 2013, her posthumously published collection *The Collected Poems of Lucille Clifton 1965–2010* (BOA) was awarded the Hurston/Wright Legacy Award for Poetry.

෨෬

The publication of this book is made possible, in part,
by the special support of the following individuals:

Anonymous
Angela Bonazinga & Catherine Lewis
Rome Celli, *in memory of Suressa Forbes*
James Long Hale
Sandi Henschel, *in memory of Anthony Piccione*
The LGBT Fund of Greater Rochester
Melanie & Ron Martin-Dent
Edith Matthai, *in memory of Peter Hursh*
Joe McElveney
Dorrie Parini & Paul LaFerriere
Boo Poulin
Steven O. Russell & Phyllis Rifkin-Russell
Allan & Melanie Ulrich
William Waddell & Linda Rubel
Michael Waters & Mihaela Moscaliuc